STREAMS OF LIVING COLOR

THE LIGHT OF HIS GLORY

MELISSA HARRIS

STREAMS OF LIVING COLOR: THE LIGHT OF HIS
GLORY

First printing 2008

Printed in the United States

Published by InstantPublisher

ISBN: 978-1-60458-391-5

DEDICATION

To God, Who Was, Is, and Is To Come.

It is an honor and my highest privilege to write for You.

To Kylie, who encourages me always, thank you

for your unwavering friendship.

To the Brim family, who adopted me as one of their own.

To Lucy, who taught me how to find that place in the Spirit.

To Mom, Charles and Melanie, who supported me
throughout my life.

To Grandma Daisy whose love never gives out or gives up.

And to all of those who will read this book,

and dare to be in The Light as He is in The Light.

"What I tell you in darkness, that speak ye in the light: and what ye hear in the ear, that preach ye upon the housetops."

MATTHEW 10:27

INTRODUCTION.

I admit it.

Sometimes, I like to eavesdrop on other people's conversations. There is much to be learned by assuming the role of the quiet observer from time to time. For instance, during the three decades that I have been a believer, I've had the opportunity to hear "church-folk" carry on some interesting dialogues with one another!

"Brother Martinez, did you know that in the Dark Ages, the Church locked all the Bibles up so that no one could read the Word?"

"I heard that once! Sister Mabel Mae, this world that we live in is getting so dark."

"Yes it is. You can even see the powers of darkness at work in that situation that I saw on the news last night. Not to mention what happened with the piano player..."

True. True. True. Although, it seems that in this time that we are living, it has become increasingly easy to be more conscious of the darkness than we are of it's opposing force. A force that is increasing by the minute, infinitely more powerful, and unquestionably worth a greater portion of our attention.

In Exodus 33:18, Moses cried out "Show me Your glory!" In response, the Lord allowed him to see Him from behind as He passed by with declarations of His Name (Exodus 34:5-6). In the same manner, I had been crying out to see a revelation of His glory- and He allowed me to see the revelation of His Light. God is faithful to reveal to us the

6

things we need to see, even when we don't know quite what it is that we are asking for!

What follows in this book is what I saw and learned in the days following that experience with God.

I had been pretty comfortable keeping this revelation of His Light to myself. I had only been released to minister on it one time over the past year, but one evening as I was staying in a hotel in Tulsa, Oklahoma, the Lord reminded me of the passage "…How shall they hear without a preacher? And how shall they preach, except they be sent?" (Romans 10:14-15).

How shall they hear?

So I began to look up scripture as it related to revelation knowledge and decreeing it on the earth. I found that there are many ways that a person can hear from the Lord- whether through reading the Word, time spent in prayer, the "inward witness" or leading, or receiving a "rhema" or spoken word that is uttered under the inspiration of the Holy Spirit.

While all these ways of receiving communication from the Lord are valid, everything that you hear or read should line up with the Scripture. This time in which we are living has been called the "Information Age." There is a veritable onslaught of worldly wisdom to be found for the seeking mind. Television guru's whose words bear more weight than the Constitution of the United States. An internet site for every topic. A magazine that promises to make you an expert in any field from making a scrapbook to flying a bi-plane. Yet, I found that the Book of Revelation says "…he that has an ear, let him hear *what the Spirit says unto the churches…*" (Rev 2:7, 17, 29, 3:6, 3:13, 22).

1 Corinthians 2:14 reads

> **But the natural man receiveth not the things of the Spirit of God: for they are foolishness unto him: neither can he know them, because they are spiritually discerned.**

And John 16:13 (Amplified) goes on to say

> **But when He, the Spirit of Truth (the Truth-giving Spirit) comes, He will guide you into all the Truth (the whole, full Truth). For He will not**

speak His own message [on His own authority]; but He will tell whatever He hears [from the Father; He will give the message that has been given to Him], and He will announce and declare to you the things that are to come [that will happen in the future].

So in light of this verse, we understand it is a priority for believers and the rest of the world to find out what the Spirit of God is saying to the churches! Both through the Bible and rhema words coming forth today.

When received, unless it's something that God is showing you for the purpose of personal instruction, it should be proclaimed to the world louder than the cable news channels can broadcast it!

Declared with confidence!

Paul prayed that "…I may open my mouth boldly, to make known the mystery of the gospel" (Ephesians 6:19).

Not only did he say that he'd make it known, but he would do it BOLDLY!

Who should he tell? Those that have an ear! They don't even need two ears according to the Book of Revelation, just one! "…Him that has *an* ear…." The Amplified Bible says "He *who is able to* hear!" Glory to God! That includes almost everyone!

So, as you read this book, open your eyes, ears and heart to what the Lord is telling us about the subject of His Light. There is a powerful prayer in Ephesians chapter 1, where the Apostle Paul prays that "The eyes of your understanding may be enlightened…" (v.18). With the awareness of that verse, and while studying the writings of the Prophet Isaiah, I came across a scripture that I felt that I needed greater insight on:

> **When the enemy comes in, like a flood the Spirit of the LORD will raise up a standard against him.**
> **–Isaiah 59:19 (punctuation change, mine).**

The meaning of the above verse can be altered depending on where the comma is placed. If the punctuation is moved to the right, it seems that the enemy can come in like a flood. If the comma is placed in the manner it appears here, then the Spirit of the Lord rises up like a flood instead.

I asked the Lord, "What is that standard? What has the power to flood?" And the answer seemed to settle deep into my spirit. Only The Light of God and The Love of God. Shining with the intensity of ten thousand suns. In this book we will focus on The Light, as there are many other excellent teaching materials available on Love.

It is my prayer that after you finish reading this book you have a new comprehension of The Light. Many people know that light is an attribute of God, but few realize that Light, Himself, is a powerful weapon of our warfare.

As in all good stories, to truly understand what is going on, we must go back to the beginning. For it was here that God set a precedent.

As a matter of fact, much to our delight, He defined the purpose and power of His Light within the first verses of the first book of the Bible.

"Who coverest thyself with light as a garment: who stretchest out the heavens like a curtain:"

PSALM 104:2

Chapter 1. What is The Light?

It is much, much more than the 60-watt bulb above your dining room table. In fact there is no comparison.

It is the Glory of God in That City.

It is the very essence of The Lamb of God.

He doesn't just *have* light, He *is* The Light.

And by virtue of Him being the Head, and believers being the Body,

We have *become* The Light.

Sounds simple enough, right? Not so fast. Just *knowing about it* doesn't mean that we actually know *enough*. Remember that many times in the Bible, the word "know" doesn't have anything to do with head knowledge of a subject- in the way that a 4th grader "knows" his or her time tables by rote memory. To "know" something in God's Word is to be intimately acquainted with it, inside and out.

It is derived from the word *ginosko*, in the Greek language, meaning to perceive, feel or to understand. In the Jewish language, it is an idiom that connotes the way a husband intimately "knows" his wife, as Adam "knew" Eve and conceived a son. It is knowledge to the point that you are almost as familiar with the subject matter as you are your own name.

Back in high school, all of the juniors had to take a test called the Armed Services Vocational Aptitude Battery (or ASVAB for short). The test was administered on behalf of the U.S. military to find out if any of the students at the school excelled in an area that would be of service to the

13

government. Now, I was sailing along on this test, breezing through the verbal questions, and even performing satisfactorily in the puzzle-solving and coding areas. Then I came to what I call the "Mechanical Nightmare" section. The first question had a picture of some type of circular saw, and it asked what the real name of this item was. Well, I no more knew it's name of than I knew my long-lost cousin who married Two-Toe Susie Mae back in 1904.

The next question showed some kind of pulley or belt system that I assumed would be used under the hood of a car. It wanted me to identify which part I should connect it to in order for the engine or windmill to supposedly start. I had no idea, I just knew that it was necessary in the scheme of things. Did it connect to the junket or radiator hose? Needless to say, I was not proving to be a very effective mechanic for Uncle Sam.

Through this experience, I learned that in order to use a tool in the natural, we need to understand several things. Primarily, we must identify what it is. Then we must know what it is used for. Lastly, and most importantly, we should learn how to use it correctly. Each of these steps is essential if we are to efficiently complete a project that we are working on.

It would make little sense to have a power drill and utilize it as a manual screwdriver. Yet that is what we, as the Body, have done with The Light.

In many instances we have divested it of it's power, and only see it as something to walk in instead of a weapon to be wielded.

In Bible college it was taught that if we were to fully understand a concept in the Word, many things must be taken into account. Of those items, The Law of First Mention is of particular importance. Simply stated- you should endeavor to find the passage in the Bible where that word or principle was first discussed. Usually, that scripture will contain a key to unlock the true intent of the subject you are studying.

So, for us to find an answer to the question, "What is The Light?" we have to go back to….the beginning.

THE POWER OF LIGHT
In most of your Bibles, Genesis 1:3 reads something like this:

And God said, 'Let there be light, and there was light.'

That sounds simple enough. God spoke, and because of His "God-ness" there was now a billion watt flaming bulb in the sky to illuminate the earth. Yet if that were the case, why would He go on to say in verses 14-16 that on the third day God created two great lights, the sun to govern the day and the moon to govern the night?

What kind of light was He speaking of in verse 3?

The English language, in all of it's complexity, is still very limited. In order to understand precisely what went on during that first day of creation, we need to engage ourselves in a little Hebrew lesson.

In verse 1 of that same chapter, we find the familiar verse

In the beginning, God created the heaven and earth.

Well, I think that is something that we can all agree on. God created the heaven and the earth. Unless you're a proponent of the Big Bang Theory. But we will continue under the assumption that you are a believer. (If not, there is a prayer on page 92 that you can pray from your heart to get you started on that path, but I digress).

Now we arrive at verse 2.

And the earth was without form, and void; and darkness was upon the face of the deep...

The Hebrew language here actually reads that the earth was "Tohu v'bohu". In utter chaos. A complete wasteland. Incredible. Did God create a spinning ball that had no order? Does He ever make something without form? Not a chance. Hebrew scholars believe that something catastrophic happened to the earth between verses 1 and 2.

Many believe that this was the time that the angel Lucifer fell from heaven and began his lease on the earth. (See Isaiah 14:12-17). In between those two short verses, it appears that a span of time elapsed in which Satan did what he does best. Steal. Kill. And Destroy. (John 10:10). Perfection was turned into a wilderness.

So God steps in and begins to restore order in the midst of chaos. In His divine tool belt, the first thing He pulls out is His most potent weapon. *Light.*

In verse 3, our Bibles read,

And God said, 'Let there be light', and there was light.

Can you imagine God on His throne saying something like that? In all of His omnipotence and power? Let there be light? It reminds me of a young boy at church who is hungry on youth night, quietly thinking "Let there be enough pizza left over so that I can have a few slices."

The original Hebrew text is much clearer, and closer to the character of God. It reads "Or, Hayah!" Translated into English, "Light, Be!" "Illumination, Be!" It was a command, spoken with much authority. He directed The Light to shine forth, and since the sun wasn't created for two more days, we understand that this was not physical light but a spiritual force. The energy of God that dispels the work of the devil and brings restoration to desecrated places.

God, in His desire to reestablish the planet, unleashed Himself and all the power that came with Him. And as Light Himself began to work, the force of the Ancient of Days overcame the powers of darkness to create an ordered world. Now, I want you to see that because God is God, He could have chosen from a variety of methods to fix the problem.

The Word says in 1 John 4:8 that God is Love. So He could have chosen to release that facet of Himself. But He didn't.

The Bible also says in John 1:1 that God is the Word. And He could have chosen to release just the Word. But He didn't.

If you read Psalm 75:7 it says that God is THE Judge. But just judging the devil at this juncture wouldn't have fixed the issue.

There was only one solution for a situation of this caliber. There was one way to desecrate the work of the enemy. Bring on The Light. For to do so is to bring God on the scene.

"…Rays of light flash from his hands, where his awesome power is hidden."(NLT)

Habakkuk 3:4

Chapter 2. MY VISION OF JESUS

I was rejoicing in song with about nine other people after a Thursday evening HopeCenter service. The pianist had been playing during the altar call, and we hadn't wanted to stop worshipping, even though it was getting late.

A lady who we had seen from time to time came in the door around 9:15 p.m. and asked for prayer for that she might be healed of pain in her throat and ears. (I remember the time because I looked at my watch when she walked in the door, and thought it was kind of late for her to be dropping by the HopeCenter).

Because I didn't feel the anointing to lay hands on her, I asked our worship leader, Sister Jackie Parker, to play a song on the piano that she had done earlier during the worship service. When she had played the song before I could feel the tangible presence of God and my hands had begun to heat up as if they were on fire.

Earlier, people had came forward for a healing line, the power of God was so strong that they fell under the power of the Holy Spirit before I had a good chance to lay hands on them and pray.

I knew we had tapped into something greater than I had experienced before. As Sister Jackie began to play the song again after service, once again I could feel the presence of God. She sang the chorus twice-

"Our God is an Awesome God

He Reigns, from heaven above

With wisdom, power and love

Our God is an Awesome God."

I walked over to pray for the lady with the throat and ear pain, and she received her healing instantly. Her voice even sounded better than it did before. This was around 9:30 p.m.

The worship leader continued to play the piano and sing the refrain of the song-

"He reigns,

He reigns,

He reigns,

Above all"

The power of the Lord was so strong that we all continued to sing and worship. I could not stand up, so I sat down in the chair that was behind me on the front row. Before she could sing the refrain again, I remember a sound like a thunderclap and I looked around, but I was not in the sanctuary of the church any longer.

The first thing that I was aware of was the music in the new place. It sounded like the melody that I had heard Sister Jackie play on the piano but even sweeter. Before me I could see what appeared to be the place where the throne of God stood, but I could not see God at all, only bright rivers of light, as if you were to stare directly into the sun. And the music that seemed to have carried me upwards continued to play in this place.

There were older men, gathered around the radiant light and they were bowing toward the ground in time with the melody. All of the men had on white robes with belts made of golden rope around their waists.

I began to back up and I looked to the right. A man also donning a white robe encrusted with jewels on the chest started to walk toward me. He had the most kind and brightly lit face I have ever seen. I asked him about the men wearing white robes near the throne of God.

He said, " They are the righteous, and chosen and faithful."

As He said this, he walked closer until he was what I would estimate to be no more than 50-100 feet away from me. His hands were at His side in fists, with what would be His palms facing me. He took one step closer and opened His fists.

When he did this it seemed that some type of brilliantly colored stones rested in both of His hands, almost the color of sapphires and rubies. Then I was no longer able to see the stones because a light began to emanate from the center of each of His hands so brightly that I could not make out anything else. The beams of light were focused directly on me, but they seemed to also make everything brighter in the whole area around Him. My words fail to describe the magnificence and complexity of the light. It was at once warm, brilliant, and mostly translucent with intertwined streams of crystal-clear colors. Hues of white, pink, purple, blue, green, orange and gold. It is indescribable by earthly standards. There is nothing on this planet I can find to compare it to. An awe-inspiring light and an inviting presence at the same time.

I asked him who he was.

He said, " I am Light. And in Me is no darkness at all."

I wanted to know specifically Who He was, and I trembled as I asked again "Who are You?"

He replied again "I AM LIGHT. And in Me is no darkness at all. And in my hands are the healings, and miracles and the very glory of God." When I heard Him say this, I understood that Jesus, Himself, was standing before me.

He asked me to lift my hands to His, and as I did The Light went into my hands and my body, and I began to tremble and shake before Him. I could feel everything that was of my flesh and not of God start to melt off of me. But it was not a scary feeling, it was warm, and I wanted to stay connected to the light.

He let go of my hands and said that I was there with Him for a reason. "As you lifted Me higher and higher, and sang songs that brought glory to Me and not yourselves, you were lifted with the songs. And as you lift Me higher and higher, by degree, you would begin to see My glory manifested in the same way- by degrees. And in that you will see the miracles you have longed for."

Then He said this, and I will try to write it down as best as I remember it.

"As The Light goes into my ministers of the gospel, it is directed to go out of my ministers of the gospel, and into the nations. The Light has shone forth in great measure in Africa and they have seen great numbers of healings and miracles. But it is because it has been commanded to shine in Africa.

And the Light is still breaking forth in Soviet Russia, even when we have said it is a dark place. The Light is Me, and I Am the Word.

And the Light has yet to fully break forth in America, because it has not been commanded to fully break forth in America."

Jesus stepped aside as if to let me look around. I could see the greenest grass, rolling hills, pathways and the most beautiful and large one, two, and three story houses. Some were tan in color, some white, some grey. Some mansions had gates in front of them, and the gates were made of different stones, and gold. All of it, the houses, gates, and trees, shone brighter than anything I have ever seen in my life. But *all* of the light was coming from Him.

It seemed as if the light coming from His hands reflected off of the light from the jewels on His chest and it in turn radiated to every single place that you could see with your eyes. He was really lighting up everything around Him.

I looked back at Him, and the light seemed to come from the inside of His being. I couldn't take my eyes off of it. It was the most inviting and bright light. Unlike anything on earth, and much brighter than the sun.

THE LIGHT OF THAT CITY.

As if He could read my mind, The Savior looked at me and said,

"The light in my hands is the Light of the city that was built foursquare. And it is the Light goes into you to equip you for the work. As a matter of fact, It is the same Light that is seated at the throne of God. I have created you exactly in my image and likeness, and humans were made to do the exact same things that I do. When I created the world, I said 'Light Be'.

From now on, when you lay hands on the sick, if you will tell the Light to be, the Light will come into that body and push out all of the darkness. Every disease, evil spirit, sickness and depression will go when the Light goes into that person. It *cannot* stay because the Light dispels darkness."

He was quiet again for what seemed like a couple of minutes and the light from His palms still seemed to be shining into my hands.

I asked Him if I could see more.

WORDS THAT ARE ALIVE.

He bent down and picked up a book that was beside Him. The book opened, and it looked like it contained familiar writings from the Bible. When He opened the book, a light shot out of the open pages and focused a powerful beam reaching much further into the sky than what I could see.

The words on the pages began to take on life and movement within that beam of gold light, and the individual letters started to circulate, as if they were swirling around a barber's pole, and they formed a sentence after a little while. The sentence said,

"This is a light that can no longer be hidden."

While He was still holding the brightly lit book, Jesus said to me,

"A new revelation of the Word will now belong to the Body, so that the Word can shine fully as it is taught in the pulpits and shared in the streets in this final hour. Some mysteries of the Word were hidden in times past. But now the revelation of the Word will be unfolded, and for the Body, the Light will fully shine. And this Light is the same Light of this city that is built foursquare."

He closed the book, and began to walk away. And in an instant I was back in the sanctuary at the HopeCenter. The worship leader was still playing the piano with her eyes closed, and her fingers looked as though they could not stop playing.

AFTERWARD.

I looked around me, and I realized that I was laying on the floor in the corner of the room. Everyone else was either seemingly paralyzed in their seats, or laying on their faces on the carpet. The lady who I had prayed for earlier was still singing songs in the Spirit and her voice was strong.

Someone whispered, "Jesus is in this place."

I could not talk, but I thought, "Oh yes! He is! They've seen Him too!"

After a few minutes I was able to regain my voice and asked them if they had seen Him just now. I believe it was Sister Angela Lansdown who said, "I can't see Him, but I know He's here. You can feel Him."

I got up from the floor where I was, and walked back to my office to write down what I had seen and heard on some scratch paper.

When I looked at the clock on my computer, it was 11:32 p.m. Two hours had gone by, and I don't remember anything besides what I saw of heaven after 9:30 p.m.

After I finished writing this down, I sat at my desk for awhile, and then I heard loud laughter coming from the sanctuary where I had left everyone. I went into the front to see what was going on, and except for Sister Jodee Snavely, who could not move from her seat, all who were still there had such a spirit of joy on them. I observed from the hallway, and the moment I stepped into the room, joy and laughter came over me, and we had a wonderful time rejoicing together in the presence of the Lord until half past midnight.

THE RESULTS.

Before this vision of the Lord, people would come forward for healing during services, as usual. We would, according to James 5:14, pray for them and rejoice over their physical, mental or spiritual restoration. After this experience with the Lord, I still make it a practice to pray for the sick, as Jesus said we should as believers. However, armed with the knowledge that He has given us the power to command the light to shine in the darkness, we began to proclaim that His light was reigning in whatever area they needed a touch from God.

Now, this is not a formula that everyone must follow. I am only speaking from my experience with Him, and moving in obedience to His Word. As we began to command the light to shine in different areas, the results were astounding.

When we prayed that the Light of God would shine forth in the drug-riddled areas of the city, methamphetamine labs that had existed for decades were busted by law enforcement.

When we declared that the Light of God must illuminate minds that were held in bondage by schizophrenia or bipolar disorder, young men and older women were able to think clearly for the first time in years. Outbursts of anger stopped, demons that were prompting people to commit suicide left, and under their doctor's supervision- many were able to stop taking their psychotropic medications completely with great success.

When we command "Light to be" in vessels that have been diagnosed with cancerous growths, spinal injuries, epilepsy, digestive disorders and chronic headaches, the bodies are made whole. Darkness, in the form of illness, is dispelled and not allowed to return.

Terri, a precious woman in our congregation, had received a diagnosis of tumors in her abdomen. The doctors told her that they would operate to remove them, but even then, the prognosis was not good. She came forward for prayer during one Thursday evening service before her pre-operative appointment. We agreed with her that disease had

32

to flee because the Light had come. When she went in to the doctor on Monday, she told him that she felt much better and could no longer feel the large tumors. He touched her stomach and could not find them either. So, in proper medical fashion, he ordered an MRI to find out what was going on.

When the images came back the next day, to his surprise, there were no growths or scar tissue from her last operation to be seen! The doctor asked Terri if she had seen another specialist or been put on a new regiment of medication by someone else. She replied, "No, but I had hands laid on me for healing last week. Do you believe in the laying on of hands for healing?"

The doctor said that he thought he believed in God before, but he would no longer doubt Him or His healing power! He cancelled Terri's surgery and told her that she wouldn't need to come back, because there was nothing wrong!

Another person had been far-sighted, and was trusting God to restore her vision. We prayed the same prayer, and from that day forward, she no longer needed her glasses.

During our nursing home ministry one Saturday, we encountered a man in his late 80's who was on his death bed. The doctor and his wife had come in to visit, and the family was told to say their goodbye's because the double pneumonia he had fought for weeks had taken it's toll on his body. When we came to his room, they told us he only had a few hours to live. The gentleman's breathing was very irregular and shallow, and his skin had taken on a pale tone. We asked if we could say a short prayer for him, and the family agreed.

I had the feeling in my spirit that this gentleman was not done with his race on earth. I spoke with authority that the Light must shine in his body, and within two hours he was up walking around and talking for the first time in a long time. The next day we received a report from the nurses at the home that he was in the dining room eating with the other residents. A few weeks later, a friend of mine was out shopping and saw this man walking around the store. To this day, he and his wife are living out the remainder of their days in health!

A sweet woman who we also met at the nursing home asked us to pray that she would have use of her hands again. She had suffered the debilitating effects of injuries sustained in a car accident, and her hands were closed in tight fists. As a result, she was unable to comb her own hair or pick up her fork at the dinner table. We asked her if she believed in the Lord Jesus, and she said that she did. I prayed with her, and her left hand began to open up immediately. Over the next couple of days, her right hand followed suit.

Ms. Phyllis' story is particularly amazing. This elderly woman very self-sufficient and living alone in her own home for years. One day in the spring, she found herself being wheeled on a stretcher into the ER, where the doctors told her that she had experienced a stroke. They did not know how much time had elapsed since the cerebrovascular accident (stroke) had occurred, so the physicians could not do much to reverse the effects of a lack of oxygen on her brain cells. It seemed that she would have to accept this limited existence.

Soon after, she was released to a residential care facility to live out the remainder of her days in a bed. When the ministry team from our church encountered her for the first time, we saw a sweet woman with white hair who tried in vain to smile at us, but seemed resigned to lay speechless in this facility for the rest of her life. She did not seem embittered in any way, but you could sense that she understood that she would no longer walk, fix her own meals or even hug her grandchildren. We told her that we would like to pray with her for healing, and weakly she offered us a one-sided smile as consent.

Our team gathered around her bed, and I gave thanks to God for hearing and answering the prayer of faith. We asked that His healing power flow through us to Ms. Phyllis' body. Then we commanded the Light of God to shine into her brain, and restore the brain cells that the neurologist thought were unsalvageable. After all, didn't He make those cells in the first place? Surely, God knew how to *remake* them!

The next time we went into the facility, a few members of my team came up to me and said "Hurry, you need to come with me! Someone wants to see you!"

I looked at them with skepticism, but shrugged my shoulders and followed the group to the end of the long, fluorescent-lit corridor. I was ushered into a familiar room, and in the bed near the window I saw a lady with beautiful white curls framing her face. She smiled brightly and waved me over to give her a hug. It took a moment to register that this was Ms. Phyllis! She sat upright, moved her arms excitedly, and said "Come here!"

You would not be able to tell by looking at her that she had been told a month before that she would never recover from the stroke! After embracing her for a long time and kissing her cheek, I backed up to look at her.

"Ms. Phyllis!" I exclaimed. "Look at you! God certainly has heard our prayer!"

"Yes, yes!" she said and held her arms up so that I could behold her restored strength.

A woman in her 40's walked into the room and introduced herself as Carol, Ms. Phyllis' daughter. She offered me her hand, and I shook it heartily.

"Hi! I've heard about you guys." She jovially remarked. "I lived out of state when Mom had the stroke, and something on the inside of me told me to move to Missouri and help take care of her. It was a step of faith, because I had no idea what to expect when I came here."

I greeted her, and told her about our first meeting with her mother.

"Yes, I've heard about that!" She responded. "I know that God has healed her, and that she is on the road to a full recovery. I got a job here so I could be near her. And I wanted to show you something, I'm glad I got the chance to meet you all."

Carol moved to retrieve an envelope from the pocket of her blue scrubs, and shuffled through several pictures that were inside.

"You see, I'm a bus driver. And when I moved here, God really blessed me with a full-time job, driving for the school district. There were 25 other people who applied on the same day I did. But I was the only one selected. So anyhow, everyday I take my camera with me to take pictures of the scenery between pick-ups." She smiled heavenward in gratitude. "I had heard that you all had prayed for her, and that The Light of God would shine in her..." With that, she slid a photograph into my hand.

"I knew He heard that prayer. I knew Mom was getting better and better everyday. Then, one day while I was driving along my route, I came to a spot that is always dark and completely shaded, I saw this light shining. There's *never* light in this spot. Never." She emphasized. In the photo, I could see densely grown trees that overhung a road on both sides, for almost fifty yards. Even though it was morning, there was very little light penetrating the vegetation. The road continued in almost complete darkness, as if it were evening instead of seven a.m. But as my eyes scanned the picture, shining through the treetops, there was a breathtaking ray of light to the right of Carol. This was no camera flash, and it wasn't natural sunlight. Beaming down onto the path before her was a shaft of intensely pure light.

"I don't know what all it means." She went on. "I just knew when I saw that light, God had heard your prayers. The feeling came over me that God was with me and Mom. Everything is going to be alright. It really is. Mom is getting out of this place."

And so it will be. Ms. Phyllis can speak. She can sit up and move her arms freely. And she will walk. Because our God is Mightier than the darkest night and the most incurable condition. Within myself, I asked the Lord why she wasn't walking right away, and immediately I felt chastened. The Holy Spirit ministered to me that her Father was on the scene, and the words regarding the lepers in Luke 17:14 were true in this case.

> **And when he saw them, he said unto them, Go shew yourselves unto the priests. And it came to pass, that,** *as they went, they were cleansed.* **(emphasis, mine).**

Her healing would be completed as she continued on. Sometimes, as ministers, we can get down on ourselves if we don't see an instant manifestation of someone's healing. But we see from this example of Jesus' ministry, at times healing is a process that must be wrought in a Believer's body as they persist in their walk of faith. Other times, it is instantaneous.

Why some manifestations of healing are immediate and others are not should not be a subject of contention. Either way, it is our endeavor to follow the command of Jesus to lay hands on the sick and see them recover. He is offering a free gift, and at times the faith to receive that gift must come by hearing more of the Word of God on the subject. (Romans 10:17). I have learned that in either case, divine healing always takes place when we ask for it, just as Jesus said it would.

As we saw what the Light of God was accomplishing, I earnestly began to pray that it would not just shine within our ministry, but also in the streets of the city. Reports began to roll in that members of our congregation were starting morning Bible studies at their jobs in which people were getting saved. Others ministered to drunks who became and stayed sober. Men and women who have been imprisoned are coming to Him and have voracious appetites for the Word of God!

Churchgoers who needed financial breakthroughs are continuing to sow their tithes and offerings, but as the Light has arisen in their lives, the harvest on their giving can no longer be hindered. These are people that did not even serve the Lord a year ago, or dare to darken the doorway of a church. Reports have come in that the day after they gave, checks for amounts that more than covered their needs have shown up in the mailbox! God is revealing Himself in the most miraculous ways. The list goes on and on, and I am still in awe of all that He is accomplishing!

Lucy McKee, someone I call my mentor and a minister whom I greatly respect, once said to me "Everyone's answer to everyone's problem is *in* Him." I now see how accurate that statement is. The answers do not lie in the worldly recognition of our ministries, how anointed you feel, simple mental agreement with the Word, or even a television psychiatrist. Every answer is proving to be found squarely within the Light of God.

I did not ask God for such a personal encounter. As a matter of fact, when I was a very young girl, I used to pray that I would not have any visions because I had a fear of the unknown. But as I grew in my relationship with Him over my teenage and young adult years, I would cry out for more of His presence in my walk, and a deeper revelation of Who He Is. So that I might not only read the Word, but understand His true character and desire for the Church, as revealed through the Bible and times of prayer.

Little did I suspect that night that it would be our worship which would lead me into place that I'd been seeking. Much is given by prayer, but a great number of our answers are received through worship. We are blessed in our pursuit of Him, but I strongly believe we are found by giving Him the glory.

Chapter 3. He is *My* Light!

If you have ever had, or known, a two-year old then you should be familiar with the word *"Mine!"*

"That's *my* truck."

"That's *my* cracker."

"That (whatever may be in a 10-mile radius) is *MINE!"*

I traveled to California not to long ago to visit my family, and among them lives my two-year old niece, Mia Angelina. She is a very sweet child, and if I do say so myself, pretty brilliant. She knows her colors, can count to ten in English and Spanish, read a few words and do simple addition.

One day while my sister, Melanie, and I were visiting my mother's house, I decided I would try out Mia's relational skills. I crouched down to her level and pointed at my mother, who also happens to be *Mia's Grammy.*

"Mia, do you know who Auntie's mommy is?" I asked her.

A perplexed look crossed her face, and she answered "No, Auntie Lissa. Who's your mommy? My mommy?"

"No, mommy is my sister. Grammy is Auntie's mommy." I told her. If I would have known what was coming next, I would have backed up a few hundred feet.

"No! No! She's not your mommy!" She screamed. "She's *MY GRAMMY! She's MY Grammy!*" Tears began to roll down her face as if I had kidnapped her favorite doll.

"Now, look what you did!" My sister said with a smile. In the background, Mia was clinging to my mother's legs while whimpering, "My Grammy. *Mine*." Of course, as all first-time grandmother's do, my mother was eating this up.

I looked at her helplessly, and she finally decided to give me a hand.

"Mia," My mother started, "Auntie Melissa is my baby like you are mommy's baby."

With that comment, Mia burst into a grievous wail with the saddest look on her face that I had ever seen on a child.

Mia launched a counter-attack. "Noooooo! Nooooo! No she's not. You're mine!"

"Oh nevermind. I am *your* Grammy. All yours. It's okay baby. It's okay." My mom consoled her, while giving me a look that told me if I was younger I would be spanked for my trespass. I realized that at this juncture in my niece's life, there was no point in trying to reason with her otherwise. I had no mother, and she had a grandmother.

It seems like we arrive at the height of possessiveness somewhere in our toddler years, and then begin the slow ascent into the concept known as "sharing." What belongs to a child seems very black and white. There are no boundaries to overstep, no societal graces to follow. They are acutely aware of what is theirs, and they are not afraid to use it to win an argument.

On the flight back to Missouri, I was thinking about this incident with my niece. While a young child must eventually learn that their name is not stamped on everything in the world, they are not completely wrong in asserting their authority when it comes down to what intrinsically belongs to them.

Dr. Billye Brim, a minister who I have had the privilege of working and traveling with, is a scholar of the Hebrew language and a friend to the Jewish people. As I was speaking to her about my research for this book, she invited me to take a look at the *Tehillim* [1]. Shame of all shames, I did not have them, so I asked to *borrow* (for an extended period of time) her daughter Brenda's set.

The *Tehillim* is the name for the Book of Psalms which has been anthologized in a set from the original Talmudic, Midrashic and Rabbinic sources in Hebrew. Since that is the language the Old Testament was originally written in, it serves as a great point of reference in comparison to our antiquated or modern English translations. I highly suggest that you buy a copy or borrow a friend's, as I did.

The passage that Dr. Brim referred me to was Psalm 27, which reads:

> **The LORD is *my* light and *my* salvation; whom shall I fear? The LORD is the strength of my life; of whom shall I be afraid? (v.1- *emphasis, mine.* No really, it's mine!)**

In The *Tehillim,* the first line of that verse simply reads, "HASHEM (the Name of God which cannot be pronounced) ORI YESHUA." My light (possessive) is as the LORD's Salvation! Whose light? *Yours.* Why would this scripture say this? Well, we can start with a little background. The Jews recite this Psalm during the Ten Days of Repentance. That might seem a little strange, since it's a Psalm that barely speaks of repentance. Yet by looking at the first verse, we can see that it is a Psalm that would help them deal with sin by proclaiming the cure for darkness in all of its forms- The Light.

A Hebrew commentary called *The Midrash* states that God provides this light in direct proportion to a person's desire for it. This applies on a personal, familial, city-wide and national level. In the vision of Jesus I had, He told me that The Light is shining in different levels on different continents. Why? It only shines in response to the call. It is certainly capable of shining everywhere, but God moves only in response to the prayer of faith. He will give it to you, and you may use it as a weapon both in your life and others, but it must be a desire that is spoken forth.

The scripture goes on to say that your light (HASHEM) is as YESHUA (or Jesus), which means *salvation*. The Light, which shines in our hearts, functions as assistance to those who, for whatever reason, are unable to help themselves. If God Himself is permeating your being, and He is the source of your strength or your children's strength, then the second part of verse 1 makes much more sense.

The LORD is the strength of my life; of whom shall I be afraid? (KJV)

or

...So why should I be afraid? (NLT)

Certainly not as a result of the devil or his powers of darkness! In the Light, there is clarity. And where there is clarity, it is much easier to be aware of Satan's devices (2 Corinthians 2:11).

King David was speaking of this concept in Psalm 119:105 when he wrote:

> **Your word is a lamp to guide *my* feet and a light for *my* path. (NLT-*emphasis, mine*.)**

He understood that the Word (which is God, see John 1:1), was not only a light in general, or something that was seen on Jesus' face on the Mount of Transfiguration. The Light is an attribute of God that belonged to David, which during his youth and his kingly reign, he prayed would illuminate his path to remove hindrances and provide assistance.

2 Corinthians 4:6 says this Light also shines in *our* hearts, so now it belongs to you! If it's in your container, then you have a right to use it! Furthermore, just as you were born to your natural mother and father, and are genetically composed of their physical attributes, you have been re-

born from above (John 3:7), and *have* your Heavenly Father's attributes! When you have children, or procreate, you release those features into another generation. Have you ever heard anyone say 'You *have* your father's nose' or, 'You *have* your mother's eyes'? Well, now you are a child of Light (1 Thes. 5:5)! This means that your spiritual genetic code, for all intents and purposes, is composed of Light and Love. Because of this, you are able to release His attributes into the generation in which you are living.

You don't have to try to shine it forth, and hope it works. It belongs to you, just as much as your nationality or your name. *Your Light* is as the Lord's salvation!

"...thou hast prepared the light and the sun"

PSALM 74:16

Chapter 4. The Light Changes The Seasons

I was in a prayer meeting in July and the word came forth that we would be coming upon a season change as the Body of Christ. A time of unprecedented manifestations of His glory, record numbers of salvations, and the free flow of miracles, signs and wonders. A time in which the Bride who is completely in love with her Bridegroom is displayed in all her splendor for the world to see!

An engaged couple, over the course of their courtship, sets a wedding date. As the days, weeks and months speed by on the way to the "big day", the seasons also change. They can feel the hot days of July and August cool down as summer gives way to fall. And soon they will see the snow and ice of winter melt as February gives heed to the spring blossoms in March. Sooner than they expected, it is time to march down the aisle!

The seasons that the Bride of Christ (2 Corinthians 11:2, Ephesians 5:31-32) walks through are viewed in light of God's timeline, and He designed the process of the Jewish marriage as a wonderful meter by which we could gauge which season we are living in.

There are seven steps in Judaism that must take place as a new covenant is being formed between a man and a woman, and we see it mirrored in the relationship between God, the Father, the Son, and the Church.

Let's look at the amazing similarities:

1. The Selection- The son chooses his perfect bride. Jesus Christ has chosen the Church.

2. Dowry is Paid- The father and son pay a dowry to the bride's family for the right to bring her into groom's family. God sent His Son Jesus to pay a price with His blood for the Bride.

3. A Gift is Given- The son gives the bride a gift, like a ring, as a pledge that he will fulfill his promise and marry her. After Jesus paid the price, he gave the gift of the Holy Spirit to the Church so she would not be comfortless in His absence.

4. Espousal- In modern day vernacular, the woman is now engaged. In the Jewish religion, this is every bit as binding as the marriage itself. She begins to wear a veil that sets her apart from other unmarried women. This is the season that the Church is in now. We are to be in a time of clear separation (also known as holiness) unto our Bridegroom. The distractions that once held us back from reaching toward the complete possession of the Lover of our Souls should become things of the past. We are now called to be His spotless Bride.

5. The Bridegroom Cometh- The son goes to the bride's home to fetch her for the wedding. Praise God, this is the next season for every believer! The Rapture of the Church! The Son, at the Father's command, is coming to get His bride.

6. He Takes Her to His Father's House- After the son goes to get his bride, he brings her back to his father's house. Likewise, when the trumpet sounds and Jesus appears, the Bride will ascend to meet Him and we will go to our Father's house-where He has prepared a place for us!

7. The Wedding Feast- Once the bride arrives at the father's house, she finds a great meal prepared for the whole family. Both families sit down and eat together in an atmosphere of celebration. John writes in Revelation 19:9 (AMP) that the Church also has a similar event to look forward to:

> **Then [the angel] said to me, Write this down: Blessed (happy, to be envied) are those who are summoned (invited, called) to the marriage supper of the Lamb....**

The Body is in a time of preparation right now, but as His Light increases in intensity- the next season will surely be unveiled, and it's our job to be aware of our wedding date. Hallelujah! He's coming for His Bride! In response to that Love, we should excitedly allow ourselves to be led day-by-day to The One who is waiting at the altar.

God is a God of details, and even though He has painted this picture of marriage, He didn't stop there.

Let's look at what God said in Genesis 1:14

> **…Let there be lights in the firmament of the heaven to divide the day from the night; and let them be for signs, and for seasons, and for days, and years.**

The word for "signs" in the passage above is actually the word "ot" (pronounced owe-t) in Hebrew. This means a signal, proof or warning. And the word "seasons" here is actually the Hebrew word "moed" which means "the appointed time, appointed meeting or set feast!"

What is our signal or warning that we have an appointed meeting? The lights! Literally, the sun, the moon and stars. Watching them and their patterns was actually a science that was ordained by God Himself, and corrupted by mankind and modern-day astrology.

Yet, that wasn't the only light He was speaking of.

In Revelation 21:23 the Word tells us

> **…The city had no need of the sun, neither of the moon, to shine in it: for the glory of God did lighten it, and the Lamb is the light thereof.**

From reading this we understand that the glory of God and the Lamb function as the light of heaven. Even greater than that, this glory *is* The Light.

By default then, when the glory of God floods this earth in a greater measure- The Light also floods the earth simultaneously, and shines brightly into the dark places. Yes, the darkness *is* getting darker, but the intensity of the Light is not only appearing brighter- it *is* going to get brighter before the Bride departs her earthly home. As a result of this increase in The Light, we will see a season change. Not only for the Church, but for the world around us.

The Natural Science Behind It All.

As the days grow shorter and nights grow longer on this earth, we see the leaf colors begin to change in the fall. No other factor- such as temperature, moisture or soil quality can affect the foliage more profoundly than the light.

The chlorophyll production slows down and eventually stops on broad-leaved plants, causing the other colors to be unmasked. The green fades into the background, and we see a vibrant palette of red, orange, and gold. The amount of light brings not only a rise or drop in the mercury on your patio thermometer, but it also brings about a change in our *visual perception* of the season.

The Light of God that is allowed to shine forth through the church will also change many things around us. Suddenly the colors that have been masked will be revealed, manifestations of miracles will spring forth, and before the Church is whisked away- the world will sit up and take notice! Why? Because *we* are in the Light as He is in the light!

When the Northern Hemisphere is tilted directly toward the light (the Sun) we experience the summer months. The opposite is true of winter. As our planet tilts away from the sun, the atmosphere grows darker and the weather turns colder.

Are you living in a spiritually dark and cold climate? Well don't just sit there and give glory to the powers of darkness in your family or city! If you're in The Light today, you have the power to do something about it! The Light changes the seasons. Use it to your advantage!

Chapter 5. Command it to Shine

But if our gospel be hid, it is hid to them that are lost: In whom the god of this world hath blinded the minds of them which believe not, *lest the light of the glorious gospel of Christ,* who is the image of God, *should shine unto them...* For God, who commanded the light to shine out of darkness, hath shined in our hearts, to give the light of the knowledge of the glory of God in the face of Jesus Christ. (2 Corinthians 4:4, 6)

When Paul was speaking about "the god of this world" in this verse, we sometimes assume that he was referring to the earth. In reality, he used the Greek word "kosmos," which means "world system." Satan is not literally parading around on the terra firma with a crown and scepter. But through this world's system that promotes greed, perverse media which can assault the senses, a culture of hostility against the simplicity of the gospel, and other forms of demonic activity, Satan has tried to subdue the church. As a matter of fact, if he can't make the church invisible, then the best he can do is to make it appear powerless in the eyes of the unbeliever.

Why would he blind the eyes of these people who are already walking in darkness? The Apostle Paul says the reason is pretty obvious.

So he can be sure that the light of the gospel can't shine unto them.

All it takes is a small amount of light to shine in a dark room and suddenly the room is no longer completely dark. But for the god of this world system, that's a big chance to take.

That a bit of illumination might leak out from the Christian television channel, or a friend at school who knows the Word? The chances of mission failure are too great for the defeated one.

So in an effort to keep the unsaved in that exact state, he places a blinder on their eyes through shame, bitterness, misunderstanding and distraction. That way if Light does come to their house, the devil figures they still can't see it.

But he's wrong. The scripture at the beginning of this chapter says that God *commanded* the light to shine. When has God ever commanded anything and it failed to happen? We'll take this a step further. Genesis 1:26-27 says that He created us in His likeness and image, with the same power in our words.

If He commanded the light to shine in the darkness and it worked, then shouldn't it work for you and I?

His only prerequisite according to Mark 11:23-24 is that we must believe that the things that we speak will come to pass, and they'll do exactly that.

The darkness cannot supercede The Light.

In any situation.

John chapter 1, verse 5 reads:

And the light shineth in the darkness, and the darkness comprehended it not.

In our English vocabulary, the word comprehend signifies that we understand something. Yet the New Testament was not written in English, it was translated from an ancient language. You will find that the word "comprehend" is actually a long Greek word (one I won't burden you with for now) that means to "seize, conquer or hold under." So the literal translation would read "The darkness cannot seize, conquer, or hold under The Light." Glory to God! It *cannot!*

One morning, before we started the HopeCenter, I was enjoying my morning prayer time. Suddenly, I found myself no longer on my living room couch, but in the midst of a vision of the city in which I live. It seemed as though a large part of the area was covered in a dark mesh that prevented the sun from filtering completely through to the residents beneath. I heard an audible voice that said "Command the light to shine *in* the city." Repeatedly I commanded it to shine over the houses, trailers, apartment homes and businesses that I could see.

Each time, a hole would appear in the thick mesh that was preventing the light from shining. Gradually, men, women and children began to come out of their homes and look up at the light as if they had never seen it before in their lives. I knew from that point on that The Light of God would be our primary tool in overcoming the strongholds in our community.

What we pray out in the spirit realm always preceeds what occurs in the natural realm. It wasn't too long after that vision that the Lord placed it on my heart to start a Food Storehouse for needy families in the community. It would be a way to demonstrate the practical love of Christ to those who did not know the Lord. All I had was a word from God, and that was all I needed.

One glorious Tuesday afternoon, I marched over to City Hall and found the Health Department. As I patiently waited for someone to help me, I sensed a great excitement in my spirit about this new venture. Little did I know that a storm cloud was moving over my parade route.

When the worker finally appeared from behind the cubicle maze, she kindly asked what type of help I was there to receive.

In my naiveté I proclaimed "I'm the Pastor at the HopeCenter and we'd like to start a food pantry in this city to benefit the poor."

I should have sensed that the tide was about to turn, but I had my word from God.

"Well," she replied, "Do you even know how you're going to fund this pantry of yours?"

"What type of building you have? Does it have sinks? Do you know they already have free food for the needy in Springfield?" She went on. And on.

I told her that we had faithful partners in the ministry who were sowing into the lives of people in this community, that we had a great building- with at least seven sinks, and yes, we did know about Springfield, which was almost 40 miles away. I asked if she could schedule a time to come to the church for a site inspection so we could proceed with our plans.

"I wouldn't try this if I were you." She warned. "If you give a man a fish, he'll eat for a day. If you teach him to fish, he'll eat for a lifetime. We don't want homeless people in this city lining up at soup kitchens. Refer them some place else." With that she disappeared back behind the counter.

Ouch. I felt like I had been punched in the stomach. We already had many programs in place that would help people get off of drugs, find jobs, find Jesus. We *were* teaching people how to fish.

How could an idea that I knew came from the Lord be dismissed so easily? The timing seemed right, and the Word guaranteed that the provision would be there.

Then I remembered the god of this world system. By stopping this outreach, he was attempting to seize The Light. The same way that he tries to seize a person's family, finances, health, and ultimately, their lives.

The writer of Ecclesiastes says in chapter 3, verse 15 (NLT) that "What is happening now has happened before...."

Satan's tricks don't change. That's why our weapons shouldn't change from the ones that God used in the Word. The devil didn't just want to steal our light at the church. In the book of Isaiah, he attempted to hijack *The Light.*

How you are fallen from heaven,

O shining star, son of the morning!

You have been thrown down to the earth,

You who destroyed nations of the world.

For you said to yourself,

'I will ascend to heaven and set my throne

above God's stars.

I will preside on the mountain of the gods far

away in the north.

I will climb to the highest heavens and be like

The Most High.'

Instead, you will be brought down to the

place of the dead, down to it's lowest depths.

(vv. 12-15 NLT)

On first glance, we see that the angel Lucifer had a tiny problem with pride. Well, maybe it wasn't so tiny.

He began to say within his own heart that he would set his dark little throne above God's. The Bible doesn't even mention that he said these words out loud. It was enough to think these things in the presence of God. We understand from reading Ezekiel 28:12-15 that he was *the* anointed cherub, with vocal chords like organ pipes and a flawless appearance. He was created to make music around the throne. He was created to stand in The Light.

Yet Isaiah writes that Lucifer did not just fall down from heaven like a skydiver, the verse says that he was *thrown down*. Some commentaries report that it all happened in less than $1/1000^{th}$ of a second.

What could promote such a quick reaction? The only possible answer is that when iniquity entered his heart, The Light that surrounds the throne dispelled the darkness faster than you can blink.

The darkness tried to seize The Light.

The Light cannot be overpowered.

The Planning Committee decided to override the Health Department in favor of the church.

Game over.

Command it to shine, and then enter into rest.

Chapter 6. The Physics of Light and The African Mine

$c = 186,000$ miles per second.

$c =$ The constant of the speed of light.

Einstein declared that "c" never changes, and that nothing can ever travel faster than it does. Or so he thought. Today scientists think that the constant isn't so constant after all.

In the 1970's, French physicist Francis Perrin began examining the uranium ore in the Oklo Mine in Gabon, Africa. When he was younger, he had been one of the first scientists to figure out how uranium played a role in a nuclear chain reaction. He studied fission- how uranium atoms were split, which releases energy and neutrons, and then how those neutrons split into more atoms again and again to create great sums of energy.

Without going into detailed physics, nuclear fission leaves a few byproducts that are a result of the extreme heat produced during the reaction[2]. As Perrin and his team examined these byproducts, they discovered that some of the atomic weights of the Oklo elements were slightly off. It seemed as though the elements in this mine were made in a different place than every other element in the world.

Now, just as we were discussing "c" at the beginning of this chapter, there is another term in physics called "alpha." Alpha is also called "the fine structure constant." It's numerical value, in case you were curious, is 1/137. If you were to study it out or insert it into a formula, it would tell you how tightly parts of an atom bind together.

The importance of alpha, according to science, is that if this number was higher or lower, atoms could never have formed. If atoms had never formed, life wouldn't exist. It is because of this mysterious "alpha" that brilliant physicists like Nobel Prize winner Richard Feymnman say that "All good theoretical physicists put this number up on their wall and worry about it…You might say the 'hand of God' wrote that number."

Well, what does that have to do with little Oklo in Africa? If alpha had once varied even a little bit, then the differing atomic weights of the elements in this mine could be explained. Maybe the atoms came together a little differently in the past.

The whole hitch in this idea is that alpha is a "fundamental constant." Like a fundamental Christian. This means that this number should never, ever, ever change. That's why it's called a…"constant." Every calculation regarding the nature of the universe and the Big Bang Theory is based on this number. And alpha doesn't stand alone. Alpha is firmly tied to other constants, and is quite significantly related to "c." The constant for the speed of light.

If alpha changed somewhere in the earth's history, then uh-oh, so did the speed of light. And if that's true, then science knows much less about the creation of the universe than they speculated.

How could the speed of light vary? At this point, scientists aren't really sure, but there is one thing that we know as believers.

He is Light, and He is a constant (James 1:17b). The Word proves that He is unchanging and unchangeable. But the force of this light is proving to be outside the limits of human measurement and constraints of our intellect.

Since He occupies all time- past, present, and future, there is a very real possibility that He could travel at 200,000 miles per second or 150 miles per minute, and His Son would still uphold the universe by the Word of His power, according to Hebrews 1:3.

> **[God] hath spoken to us by his Son, whom he hath appointed heir of all things, by whom also he made the worlds; Who being the brightness of his glory, and the express image of his person, and upholding *all things* by the Word of his power.... [emphasis, mine].**

When God spoke "Light Be" in Genesis 1:3, the strength of Jehovah moved across this planet to restore order in the midst of absolute chaos. Alternately, when David sang in Psalm 119:105 "Thy word is a lamp unto my feet, and a light unto my path," he needed just enough illumination to rule his kingdom righteously. It took the power of God to accomplish both tasks, but in varying degrees.

Should He fully release the Light of His Glory on this earth, there is a great chance that man in his fallen state could not continue to live. For what flesh could stand continually in the glory of God? And so in His infinite love, we experience a measure of His presence until we are caught up to meet Him in the air.

Love just might be the variable in the constant that science has not accounted for.

"...Anyone who has seen me has seen the Father."

-Jesus Christ

JOHN 14:9 NLT

Chapter 7. Reflection and Representation

Jesus was a reflection of God. He wasn't just His royal ambassador who was sent to represent Him on the earth. He was sent, as a man, to *be* Him on the earth. Though the two words both start with "r" they aren't the same thing.

Webster's dictionary defines a representation as *the action of one person standing in for another so as to have the rights or obligations of the person being represented.*

While a reflection means *the exact production of an image by or as if by a mirror.*

Jesus said in John chapter 5, verse 19

I tell you the truth, the Son can do nothing by Himself. He does only what he sees the Father doing. Whatever the Father does, the Son also does. (NLT)

In essence, Jesus was saying that he was a mirror image of His Father. If you stand in a mirror and move your arm, then your reflection in the mirror moves it's arm. If you close your mouth, then your reflection closes it's mouth. The reflection works in concert with you, and cannot function apart from you.

This is a great contrast to a representation.

A founder of a corporation cannot be in a multitude of places at one time, so he or she hires representatives. These representatives have been trained by a company at one time or another, and have knowledge of the corporate vision and products. Their job does not require them to look or speak like the founder, only to represent him and his line of "quality products" to customers who may be interested in buying the goods. If the customer has seen you, that doesn't mean by any stretch of imagination, that they have seen the president of the company.

Many times, as believers, we feel that it is our job to represent God, and His Light, to our families, co-workers, and classmates. Lawyers are sometimes called "representatives", because they stand in front of the judge on our behalf and plead our case. But we all know, that depending on how good the attorney is, some cases are lost and some are won. God is not searching the earth for a man or woman to defend Him, prosecute for Him, or sell Him to the masses- although sometimes we can feel it is our "Christian duty." He is enough in and of Himself. Let's look at what it says in Isaiah 40, verses 13-14:

Who hath directed the Spirit of the LORD, or being His counselor hath taught Him?

With whom took he counsel, and who instructed him, and taught him in the path of judgment, and taught him knowledge, and shewed him the way of understanding?

What God has actually called us to do is to *reflect* His Light. This is a much more effective way of showing the world all the love that He offers. He has placed light within us, but it's not just so that we can show people where they can get their own supply by ordering it from our catalogs (translated: Bibles). Neither was it designed to be stockpiled inside the churches and gospel tents where others can hear about it in a 30-minute time-share presentation. We receive it, and then we are to shine it forth so others can see the Father. Like the moon, we have no light apart from the sun, but as we line up with it, we begin to reflect it's pure brilliance to the world. This happens on a day-by-day basis. When we awaken, we declare that His Light is shining in our cities. When we go to work we speak to others in love, because love has arisen in our hearts by the Holy Ghost. When we go about our business, we do it in a manner that brings Him glory. As we turn in at night, we continue our fellowship with Him. As we do this others are attracted to God in you and will believe. Simply because the reflection of His Light is a power that cannot be ignored.

It is at once a simple and a magnificent challenge to become a reflection of God. Continually, day and night, we should seek to be in His presence. A reflector is only effective as long as light is shining on it. That does not mean that we must live with our "head in the clouds" but that we are perpetually aware of God and our communion with Him in everything we do.

The angels, who know no sin, dwell continually in God's presence. Yet, the Word tells us that every time they orbit His throne they see a new facet of Him. The elders never tire of bowing to worship The Beginning and The End of all things. In contrast, we as humans, who are in dire need of His Light, come to stand in awe of His glory and majesty for a couple of hours on Sunday and maybe once or twice a day, and deem ourselves "filled up."

As the army of the Living God, we send forth people into the battlefield that have at one time or another been with Jesus, but have grown dim from being apart from Him. If we, as the Body of Christ, are to reflect Jesus to the world, and wish to do it in a greater way than wearing a bracelet with a fish imprinted on it, we are going to have to start abiding. As we stay in line with the Source of Light, God and the magnitude of His power will be brilliantly displayed as we command it to shine from within us.

Chapter 8. Jenny's Song

A friend of mine from Fort Worth, Texas is gifted in the area of singing and songwriting. One evening after I preached at a small church in Collinsville, Oklahoma on my vision of Jesus, I asked her if she had a song to close out the service. She said that she did, and it would go well with the message. The Lord had given it to her the year before, and she had not yet shared it with me. As she began to sing the song and strum quietly on the guitar, The Presence of God became tangible in the room and the youth began to fill the altar.

I was overcome with wonder at the lyrics because they so perfectly described the way in which His Light is to shine forth into the world through the Body! I asked her to sing the song again in Branson, Missouri during a service and it had the same effect. The Presence of God showed up!

One day, she emailed me the words, whether out of my incessant hounding or as a friendly gesture, I do not know. As I read over them, it was clear to me that Jenny had come into an intimate knowledge of The Light of God, and it's role in our lives.

As a toddler, Jenny Kutz, a granddaughter of Brother Kenneth and Sister Gloria Copeland, survived a serious vehicle accident that almost took her life. Though she was too young to remember all of the details of that day, I believe that there was an impartation of His Light and Love into her spirit. As you read over the account of how she received the words to this song, ask Him to show you how you can be an effective conductor of His Power in your family, school, church, job or city!

IN JENNY'S WORDS.

The best songs you can write and sing are the songs straight from heaven. The songs that you get when you are in the presence and Glory of the Lord. "You are my Light" was one of those songs.

I was leading worship with some children at our kid's church camp and began singing in the Spirit and singing with our understanding. It was then that the Lord gave me this chorus:

> *"You are my Light. You are my Light. Shine on me.*
> *Shine through me. I will not hide. I will not hide.*
> *Shine on me. Shine through me."*

It was then that I began to sing it out, and the kids joined in. Those words were all I had of the song: a simple chorus, yet one that brought the children into the Holy presence of God. What an honor!

When I got back home from camp, I did not work or toil to get the rest of the lyrics, but the Blessing dropped them on my heart. There is no need to toil in song writing. The Holy Spirit knows what songs are needed on the earth. That's why we must trust Him to lead us and fill our mouth with His words, as it says in Jeremiah 1:9.

I wrote the song in 5 minutes. Let me correct myself, it took the Holy Spirit 5 minutes for me to write that song down. I find that the songs that are divinely inspired come that quickly. The Lord knows what He wants.

I kept that song hidden in my heart for a couple years, actually. Two times I played it for a few people, but it was not time for the song to be revealed so it did not have the impact the Lord intended for it. It was not until Pastor Melissa revealed the vision the Lord have given her about Jesus and the Light that the Holy Spirit prompted me to go up on the platform. I knew that He was leading me to play the song that had been in the depths of my heart for all those years.

The Lord makes everything beautiful in its time. And it was the time.
What an honor to be a part of this huge plan God has.
What an honor.

YOU ARE MY LIGHT

The night is overcome by
The Light
I am not scared, I am not
scared.
Your Love puts darkness
aside
I am not scared, I am not
scared.
You've placed Your Light
in me
So all men can see that

You are my Light
You are my Light
You shine on me
Shine through me
I will not hide
I will not hide
You shine on me

Shine through me
Your Word tells me to go
To the nations, To the
nations
My heart is to tell all that I
know
To the nations, To the
nations
May they see my good
deeds
And give You the glory

Light Be
In me
Light Be
In Me

©*JENNY KUTZ*
06/02/06

81

"…in thy light shall we see light."

PSALM 36:9

Chapter 9. Scripture Study- Light in The Word

If you were to look up every occurrence of the word "light" in the King James Version of the Bible, it might take you a few days, and you would find it mentioned close to 272 times in 235 verses. Most of the time, when the Word speaks of Light, it is referring to *Or,* which is the Light of God. Yet, several verses speak about different *types* of light.

Here, I've included quite a few different scriptures for your reference and study. In the first five, you will see the same word "light" in English, but with several distinct Hebrew meanings. For the most part, unless otherwise noted, the rest of the scriptures here have to do specifically with the Light of Jehovah, or the Light *that is* Jehovah.

Genesis 1:3

And God said, Let there be light: and there was light. (The Hebrew word for light here is *or*- light of life, light of prosperity, light of His face (figuratively), Jehovah as Israel's light).

Genesis 1:16

And God made two great lights; the greater light to rule the day, and the lesser light to rule the night: [he made] the stars also. (The Hebrew word here is *ma'or*- light, or luminary instrument).

Numbers 8:2

Speak unto Aaron, and say unto him, When thou lightest the lamps, the seven lamps shall give light over against the candlestick. (The Hebrew word here is *Or-Niphal,* a noun and verb combined to describe what the subject does- to be illuminated, to become lit up).

2 Samuel 21:17

But Abishai the son of Zeruiah succoured him, and smote the Philistine, and killed him. Then the men of David sware unto him, saying, Thou shalt go no more out with us to battle, that thou quench not the light of Israel. (The Hebrew word here is *niyr*- the lamp. An item which gives light to it's surrounding area).

2 Samuel 23:4

And [he shall be] as the light of the morning, [when] the sun riseth, [even] a morning without clouds; [as] the tender grass [springing] out of the earth by clear shining after rain. (This is *or-* the same Light of Jehovah as in Genesis 1:3).

Job 3:4

Let that day be darkness; let not God regard it from above, neither let the light shine upon it. (This is the Hewbrew word *n'harah-* daylight).

Job 22:28

Thou shalt also decree a thing, and it shall be established unto thee: and the light shall shine upon thy ways. (This is *or-* the same Light of Jehovah as in Genesis 1:3, as is the Light in most of the verse to follow).

Job 24:13

They are of those that rebel against the light; they know not the ways thereof, nor abide in the paths thereof.

Job 24:16

In the dark they dig through houses, [which] they had marked for themselves in the daytime: they know not the light.

Job 29:3

When his candle shined upon my head, [and when] by his light I walked [through] darkness;

Job 38:19-20

Where [is] the way [where] light dwelleth? and [as for] darkness, where [is] the place thereof, That thou shouldest take it to the bound thereof, and that thou shouldest know the paths [to] the house thereof?

Psalm 27:1

The LORD [is] my light and my salvation; whom shall I fear? the LORD [is] the strength of my life; of whom shall I be afraid?

Psalm 36:9

For with thee [is] the fountain of life: in thy light shall we see light.

Psalm 37:6

And he shall bring forth thy righteousness as the light, and thy judgment as the noonday.

Psalm 43:3

O send out thy light and thy truth: let them lead me; let them bring me unto thy holy hill, and to thy tabernacles.

Psalm 74:16

The day [is] thine, the night also [is] thine: thou hast prepared the light and the sun. (Light here is *ma'or*- a luminary body, and sun is *shemesh*- literally the sun. Some commentaries read "He has prepared the moon and the sun.").

Psalm 104:2

Who coverest [thyself] with light as [with] a garment: who stretchest out the heavens like a curtain.

Psalm 112:4

Unto the upright there ariseth light in the darkness: [he is] gracious, and full of compassion, and righteous.

Psalm 119:105

Thy word [is] a lamp unto my feet, and a light unto my path.

Psalm 119:130

The entrance of thy words giveth light; it giveth understanding unto the simple.

Psalm 148:3

Praise ye him, sun and moon: praise him, all ye stars of light.

Ecclesiastes 2:13

Then I saw that wisdom excelleth folly, as far as light excelleth darkness.

Ecclesiastes 11:7

Truly the light [is] sweet, and a pleasant [thing it is] for the eyes to behold the sun:

Isaiah 2:5

O house of Jacob, come ye, and let us walk in the light of the LORD.

Isaiah 9:2

The people that walked in darkness have seen a great light: they that dwell in the land of the shadow of death, upon them hath the light shined.

Isaiah 10:17

And the light of Israel shall be for a fire, and his Holy One for a flame: and it shall burn and devour his thorns and his briers in one day; (The word fire here is *'esh* in Hebrew, literally this can be a normal fire or a supernatural fire which accompanies God. Our word "flame" here is actually the Hebrew word *lehabah*- the flame on the tip of the weapon or head of a spear.)

Isaiah 45:7

I form the light, and create darkness: I make peace, and create evil: I the LORD do all these [things]. (The word *form* here means to create or pre-ordain).

Isaiah 58:8

Then shall thy light break forth as the morning, and thine health shall spring forth speedily: and thy righteousness shall go before thee; the glory of the LORD shall be thy rereward. (This verse suggests that the light has the capability to break forth, which comes from the Hebrew *baqa*. This is a powerful term meaning to split, cleave, break open, break through, rip up, and break up).

Isaiah 60:1

Arise, shine; for thy light is come, and the glory of the LORD is risen upon thee. (When Isaiah writes *shine* here,

87

he is using the Hebrew word that means *to become light.*
Literally translated it would read- Become light, for The
Light of Jehovah has come!)

Isaiah 60:20

**Thy sun shall no more go down; neither shall thy moon
withdraw itself: for the LORD shall be thine everlasting
light, and the days of thy mourning shall be ended.**

Daniel 2:22

**He revealeth the deep and secret things: he knoweth
what [is] in the darkness, and the light dwelleth with
him.**

Daniel 5:14 [King Nebuchadnezzar speaking to Daniel]

**I have even heard of thee, that the spirit of the gods [is]
in thee, and [that] light and understanding and excellent
wisdom is found in thee.**

Hosea 6:5

**Therefore have I hewed [them] by the prophets; I have
slain them by the words of my mouth: and thy
judgments [are as] the light [that] goeth forth.** (*Goes
forth* is the Hebrew *yatsa*- to proceed or move toward
something. This implies that the Light is not stationary, in
fact, it is propelled toward something).

Micah 7:9

**I will bear the indignation of the LORD, because I have
sinned against him, until he plead my cause, and
execute judgment for me: he will bring me forth to the
light, [and] I shall behold his righteousness.**

Habakkuk 3:4

And [his] brightness was as the light; he had horns [coming] out of his hand: and there [was] the hiding of his power. (The word *horns* here is the Hebrew *qeren-* which interestingly enough means strength or rays of light. The word *hiding* is the Hebrew word *chebyown,* meaning place of concealment or hiding. His strength is concealed in the light of His hands, as I saw in the vision of Jesus).

Matthew 4:16

The people which sat in darkness saw great light; and to them which sat in the region and shadow of death, light is sprung up. (The Greek word for darkness is *skotos-* of darkened eyesight or blindness, of ignorance respecting divine things. The Greek word for "sat" -is *kathemai-* to have a fixed abode or to dwell there. From this we understand that this region which Jesus visited dwelled continually in this state of ignorance respecting divine things. Does that sound like any place that you might know of?

Further, in this verse the word "shadow" is translated *skia* in Greek, and it is defined as *a shade that intercepts light.* Since Light cannot be intercepted, this shade is nothing more than a smoke screen!)

Matthew 5:14

Ye are the light of the world. A city that is set on an hill cannot be hid.

Matthew 5:16

Let your light so shine before men, that they may see your good works, and glorify your Father which is in heaven. (Like Psalm 27:1, "you are *my* light", this light is possessive. Literally translated *"Let this light, which is yours, give light."*)

Matthew 10:27

What I tell you in darkness, [that] speak ye in light: and what ye hear in the ear, [that] preach ye upon the housetops. (This darkness is the Greek word *skotia*, a darkness that is in want of light).

Matthew 17:2

And [Jesus] was transfigured before them: and his face did shine as the sun, and his raiment was white as the light.

Luke 1:78-79

Through the tender mercy of our God; whereby the dayspring from on high hath visited us,

To give light to them that sit in darkness and [in] the shadow of death, to guide our feet into the way of peace. (The Greek word for dayspring is *anatole*- which means a rising, as of the sun and stars from the east. When Luke speaks of this light guiding our feet, it is the Greek term *kateuthyno*, which signifies the removal of hindrances that would come to a person).

Luke 2:32

A light to lighten the Gentiles, and the glory of thy people Israel.

Luke 8:16/11:33

No man, when he hath lighted a candle, covereth it with a vessel, or putteth [it] under a bed; but setteth [it] on a candlestick, that they which enter in may see the light.

Romans 13:12

The night is far spent, the day is at hand: let us therefore cast off the works of darkness, and let us put on the armour of light. (Armor here is the Greek word *hoplon*. It denotes an arm or weapon used in warfare. It's time for us to pick up this weapon!)

2 Corinthians 4:4

In whom the god of this world hath blinded the minds of them which believe not, lest the light of the glorious gospel of Christ, who is the image of God, should shine unto them. (This passage speaks of the darkening of the minds- through distraction, bitterness and misunderstanding- of those who have no faith in God. Satan tries this tactic as an attempt to prevent the illumination of the Good News from beaming down upon them).

2 Corinthians 4:6

For God, who commanded the light to shine out of darkness, hath shined in our hearts, to [give] the light of the knowledge of the glory of God in the face of Jesus Christ.

Ephesians 5:8

For ye were sometimes darkness, but now [are ye] light in the Lord: walk as children of light:

Ephesians 5:14

Wherefore he saith, Awake thou that sleepest, and arise from the dead, and Christ shall give thee light. (The light here is *epiphausko* in Greek- Divine truth poured upon you, as the sun gives light to us as we are awakened from sleep).

Colossians 1:12

Giving thanks unto the Father, which hath made us meet to be partakers of the inheritance of the saints in light.

1 Thessalonians 5:5

Ye are all the children of light, and the children of the day: we are not of the night, nor of darkness.

1 Timothy 6:15-16

Which in his times he shall shew, [who is] the blessed and only Potentate, the King of kings, and Lord of lords;

Who only hath immortality, dwelling in the light which no man can approach unto; whom no man hath seen, nor can see: to whom [be] honour and power everlasting. Amen.

1 Peter 2:9

But ye [are] a chosen generation, a royal priesthood, an holy nation, a peculiar people; that ye should shew forth the praises of him who hath called you out of darkness into his marvelous light.

1 John 1:5

This then is the message which we have heard of him, and declare unto you, that God is light, and in him is no darkness at all.

1 John 1:7

But if we walk in the light, as he is in the light, we have fellowship one with another, and the blood of Jesus Christ his Son cleanseth us from all sin.

1 John 2:8

Again, a new commandment I write unto you, which thing is true in him and in you: because the darkness is past, and the true light now shineth.

Revelation 21:23

And the city had no need of the sun, neither of the moon, to shine in it: for the glory of God did lighten it, and the Lamb [is] the light thereof.

Salvation: Let it shine in YOUR heart.

Friend, if you are reading this book and you would like to be delivered from the power of darkness and translated (or moved to) the kingdom of His dear Son (Colossians 1:13), and be assured that heaven will be your eternal home, I invite you to say a simple prayer with me.

I guarantee that your life will change, if only you will let the Word of God work mightily in your heart. This same Word says that there is *only one way* to come to God, and it is through Jesus Christ. Jesus says in John 14:6 "I am The Way, The Truth, and The Life. No man comes to the Father but by me." Living a good life or attending a religious

94

service will not save you or I from hell and make us Christians, no more than sitting down in a garage would make us a car. We must simply come to Him, through Jesus.

The most wonderful news is that while we were still sinners (Romans 5:8) Christ died for us! He did not come to destroy our lives, but to save them! (Luke 9:56). His blood was shed so that our failures would be covered, and once again man could approach God without shame.

Romans 3:23 says that we have all sinned and fallen short of the Glory of God. And Romans 6:23 goes on to say that the price of this sin is death, *but the gift of God* is eternal life through Jesus Christ our Lord! Praise God! Salvation is a gift which is for every man, woman or young person on this earth. That means that it's free and it's for you! All you have to do is accept it. The devil might want you to think that you have to pay a price for the things that you have done in the past, but friend, the price has already been paid through the cross of Jesus!

Our Heavenly Father has made it so easy to come to Him and receive the full assurance that all is forgiven, and we can stand before His throne spotless- as new creatures! Romans 10:9 says "If you will confess with your mouth that Jesus is Lord, and believe in your heart that God raised Him from the dead, you will be saved." That's all it takes! Saying aloud with your mouth, what you believe already in your heart. I know that the Holy Spirit has led you this far, and I ask you to take one more step and read this prayer aloud wherever you are.

Dear Heavenly Father,
I thank you for loving me, and bringing me the Truth of Your Word. I do believe that Jesus Christ died on the cross for all of my sins, and that you raised Him from the dead on the third day. I ask you to be the Lord of my life from this day forward. Teach me how to walk and talk with You everyday. Thank you for forgiving me and giving me a fresh start.
In Jesus' Name. Amen.

Welcome to God's family! That's all it takes. Mark this day as a turning point in your life! I encourage you to find a good church in your area that will help you grow and understand the Word. Connect with other believers who can encourage you as you start out on this powerful journey.

If you prayed this prayer today, we would like to send you free materials to help you in your walk with God. Please write us at:

The HopeCenter
c/o Melissa Harris Ministries
P.O. Box 675
Branson, MO 65615

BIBLIOGRAPHY.

1. Feuer, Rabbi Avrohom Chaim. *Tehillim / A New Translation With a Commentary Anthologized from Talmudic, Midrashic and Rabbinic Sources.* Mesorah Publications, Ltd., 1985-2001.

2. Kean, Sam. *Mental Floss "Nice Try, Einstein."* Mental Floss, LLC. Sept-Oct 2008.